MAIN PERMANENT 91309 X √

c. 1

JB
DARROW Faber, Doris
F Clarence Darrow:
defender of the people

CLARENCE DARROW:
Defender Of The People

by Doris Faber   illustrated by Paul Frame

Prentice-Hall Inc., Englewood Cliffs, N.J.

for Annie Faber

Library of Congress Catalog Card Number: 65-11774

Printed in the United States of America

J   13505

Prentice-Hall International, Inc., *London*
Prentice-Hall of Australia, Pty., Ltd., *Sydney*
Prentice-Hall of Canada, Ltd., *Toronto*
Prentice-Hall of India (Private) Ltd., *New Delhi*
Prentice-Hall of Japan, Inc., *Tokyo*

Contents

Other P-H Books by Doris Faber:

Horace Greeley: The People's Editor
The Life of Pocahontas
Robert Frost: America's Poet

1.

"What's a Lawyer?"

When Clarence Darrow was twelve years old, his mother sewed him his first pair of long pants. Then, in September of 1869, he started going to the Academy on the hill. And his father rejoiced.

"Now you will learn Latin!" Mr. Darrow said.

"But I won't have any use for Latin," Clarence protested. "Only foreigners speak it. How many people do you hear speaking Latin here in Kinsman?" Kinsman was the small town in Ohio where Clarence was growing up.

Mr. Darrow shook his head sadly. "Latin has been a dead language for more than a thousand years," he said. "You don't learn it to speak it. But knowing it, you have the key that unlocks treasures of the mind."

Now it was Clarence's turn to shake his head. His father certainly did have some peculiar ideas! Learn a language that nobody ever talked? That sounded plain foolish. For his own part, Clarence would much rather have stayed on in the one-room district school—and spend most of his energy playing baseball.

But Clarence never thought of objecting seriously. He admired his father too much to do that—even though he knew Pa was more than somewhat different from other men in town.

Amirus Darrow, Clarence's father, loved reading the way Clarence loved baseball. There were shelves of books in every room, piles of books on tables and on the floor. Not that the Darrows were rich. The son of a plain New England farmer who had moved to Ohio, Amirus earned hardly enough to support his wife and seven children by working as a carpenter and undertaker. Yet, somehow, he always managed to buy books.

Once as a young man he had studied to become a minister. But he found that he could not preach because he could not believe in everything that his church taught. Indeed, he came to oppose any organized form of religion—and this, above all else, set him apart in church-going Kinsman.

Not only did Mr. Darrow refuse to go to church, but he

also always seemed to support the unpopular side of any question.

"Do you suppose if we all took to voting with the Democrats, Amirus, that you would vote Republican?" a neighbor once asked him.

"More than likely," Mr. Darrow said good-naturedly.

Clarence really did not mind too much when his father urged him to keep reading. He was curious about many subjects—but some of the books that his father suggested bored him stiff. He preferred to pick and choose what interested *him*.

On the whole, Clarence and his father got along very well, but there was one slightly sore point between them.

"Whatever gave you the notion to call me 'Clarence'?" the son once asked his father.

Mr. Darrow smiled. "I do believe that was the name of a handsome young man in a book your Ma happened to be reading near the time when you arrived," he said. "I didn't see the harm of pleasing her by giving you the name."

"Well, at least it's saved me from other kinds of troubles," Clarence said. "The other boys can never think up a nickname half as silly as my own name—they just call me 'Clarence,' and I'm used to that."

Then the father and son both smiled.

Not only in his own family, but also in his dealings with other people, Mr. Darrow was so gentle and kindly that, despite all of his odd ideas, everybody liked him. They even thought it fitting that in a town of square white houses—Amirus Darrow had managed to find an *octagonal,* or eight-sided, house for his family!

And many of his neighbors now and then had a hidden little feeling that he might be right about at least *some* of his notions. After all, hadn't he been strong against slavery, long before most other folk had felt it was wrong? Clarence, who had been born on April 18, 1857, could himself faintly remember escaped slaves being sheltered in their house.

But Clarence had very little interest in his father's ideas or his books—until the Fourth of July when he was fourteen.

All morning, he had been rushing around with the other boys, shooting off firecrackers and generally making a lot of noise. The Fourth had always been his favorite holiday. But somehow this year it did not seem as splendid as usual. When his sister, Jenny, came to say that he was wanted at home, he did not mind walking back with her. As they passed by the hotel on the east side of the town square, a smart horse and buggy was pulling up.

"Guess that's the speaker for this afternoon," Clarence told Jenny.

She nodded. Ten-year-old Jenny was the closest to him in the family; the others were almost all babies, or else just about grown up already—like Everett and Mary who were away at college.

"Those are nice horses," Clarence remarked. "He must be rich, that lawyer from the city."

"What's a lawyer?" Jenny asked.

Clarence stopped walking for a minute. "A lawyer?" he repeated, and frowned. "A lawyer is a man who knows all about laws. From the look of that buggy, he must be some sort of great man."

"Why don't you be a lawyer, Clarence?"

"What an idea!" he said. "But I wonder what you have to study to be a lawyer. And does it take much brains?"

In the confusion of packing up picnic baskets and helping to carry them down to the park by the river, Clarence quite forgot about this conversation. Then, after the brass band came out and played several selections, old Squire Allen stood up on the platform and put on his gold-rimmed spectacles.

"Friends and fellow citizens," he said, "may I present the speaker of the day . . ."

At the sight of such a great man—a lawyer from the

county seat twenty miles away—Clarence remembered Jenny's question: *What's a lawyer?* Well, a lawyer was a man who didn't seem the least bit scared to stand up before the whole crowd. He was a man wearing nicer clothes than any of the people in his audience. His boots were about as shiny as mirrors. Clarence glanced down at his own bare toes, and sighed. Now would it be worth the effort, becoming a lawyer?

2.

Debating

"Listen to that Darrow boy!" Old Squire Allen shook his head in amazement. "He certainly does have the trick of speaking on his feet."

"But the things he says!" Mrs. Allen shook her head disapprovingly. "That it's wrong to blame poor people for stealing, and instead of putting them in jail, we should be kind to them and teach them a trade so they can earn enough not to have to steal. *Have* to steal! Now I call that dangerous nonsense."

The white-haired squire smiled at his wife. "Don't take on so," he said. "You know as well as I do that Clarence is a fine lad. It's only natural, with a father like Amirus, that he has some peculiar ideas. But, shhhh! I

12

want to hear what Farmer Porter's son will say to knock down Clarence's argument."

Like almost everybody else who lived in Kinsman, Squire and Mrs. Allen were spending Saturday evening listening to a debate. Week after week, folks from the town and from farms for miles around gathered on Saturday nights in the big barn on the Allen property. They clapped and laughed and had an all-around good time as neighbors argued out loud on one subject or another— such as "Is Religion Necessary?" or "Is Civilization a Failure?"

Now Clarence was nineteen, and debating practically every Saturday night. "You can always count on that Darrow boy," people said. "He'll take the wrong side on any question. There's nobody else who would do it, not even his Pa. But he can speak a piece so convincingly, he makes you wish you could agree with him."

As for Clarence himself, he thoroughly enjoyed the debating.

"I like to stand up and face the crowd," he told Jenny. "To tell the truth, I like the show of it. It's exciting, having every eye on you—even if they're all against you!" And he grinned.

But almost as much as the debating, Clarence enjoyed the square dancing that followed it. There was a pink-

cheeked girl from Berg Hill who came over most Saturday evenings. When pretty Jessie Ohl walked into the barn, Clarence always felt an extra excitement.

"Did you agree with what I had to say about taxes?" Clarence would tease her as they twirled to the tunes of a squeaky fiddle.

"Oh, Clarence!" Jessie tossed her head. "You know I don't understand anything about taxes."

Still, even if she had very little interest in the important matters he debated, Clarence became increasingly interested in Jessie. And, tall and skinny though he was, Clarence had a nice face. It was hard not to like him. Jessie clearly did like him. Soon it was accepted that they were always partners in the dancing, and people thought they would marry in a few years. On other questions about his future, though, Clarence had few clear ideas.

His mother had died when he was fourteen. That blow had brought him even closer to his father. But Amirus, as he grew older, grew more dreamy and absorbed in his books. "You must go to college," he had murmured to Clarence, without seeming to realize how much money this would cost.

At the age of sixteen, Clarence had gone off to Allegheny College in Meadville, Pennsylvania. But money was scarce—"And I must admit I'm not doing much besides playing baseball," Clarence wrote to his sister. So after a year, he quit.

He had then tried house-painting and factory work before deciding, within a few months, that some more bookish sort of life was what he wanted. But exactly what could he do? While wondering, he was offered a job. At the age of seventeen, Clarence had become a teacher!

His pupils were the fifty-odd boys and girls who attended the one-room school in a village three miles from Kinsman. For three winters, he drilled them in reading, writing and arithmetic—and wondered what his next step should be. He could never support a wife on the thirty dollars a month he made teaching, so sooner or later he would have to settle on something else. But what?

Then his oldest brother, Everett, came home on a visit. *He* settled the question while they walked home together from a Saturday night debate.

"Clarence, you like books," Everett said briskly. A book-lover himself, Everett had gone through college and was now teaching in a high school in Chicago.

Clarence nodded. Indeed he did like books. Many nights, he sat up almost until dawn, reading by the light of a kerosene lamp—reading history, poetry, all sorts of books that took his fancy.

"I've heard you debate," Everett went on. "You can think clearly and to the point. You're good at speaking on your feet. You've got the kind of winning way that people like. You're a born lawyer!"

Clarence somehow could not admit to his brother that for years he had dreamed of being a lawyer—but that in the cold light of day he realized he could never do it. "It's too much like work to get to be a lawyer," he told Everett instead. "Besides, it costs money that I don't have. So I reckon I'll not try it."

"I think you should," Everett said. "In fact, I'm going to see that you do. I have money in the bank. It's yours —to pay for law school."

Clarence felt tears in his eyes. "Thanks, Ev," he said.

3.

Horse Trades

"Good luck to you, young man," the lawyer with the black beard said.

Feeling slightly dazed, Clarence let his hand be shaken. So this was all there was to it. Answer a few questions thrown out by three lawyers sitting around a table —and then congratulations! At the age of twenty-one, Clarence Darrow was a lawyer!

Of course, he had studied hard during the year he had spent at the law college in Ann Arbor, Michigan. Then, to keep from using up all of Everett's savings, he had done his second year of studying on his own, while working as a clerk in a law office in Youngstown, Ohio. He had just passed his law examination there.

"Are you going to set up in practice here?" the black-bearded gentleman now asked him.

"No, sir. I plan to open an office closer to home." What Clarence did not add was that in a city with twenty thousand people—for that was the size of Youngstown in 1878 —he could not be comfortable. A place like Kinsman, with its four or five hundred residents, was more what he was used to. But there would be very little lawyering business in a town of that size. So he had settled on practicing law in the town of Andover, about ten miles from Kinsman. Andover was not much bigger than Kinsman, but it was more centrally located in the prosperous farm country of northern Ohio.

Here he rented three tiny rooms up one flight of stairs from a shoe shop. These rooms became his home—and his office. After putting a sign in his front window, he sat back to wait for people to come and give him some kind of work to do.

What kind of work? In a small town like Andover, there were comparatively few problems that people would bring to a lawyer. If a farmer poured water into the milk he brought to market—and a storekeeper suspected that the milk had been watered—then the storekeeper might have the farmer brought before a justice of the peace and charged with cheating. Then the storekeeper—and the farmer—would both need a lawyer to help them. Should there be a dispute about where the boundary lay between two farms, then both farmers involved would need a lawyer. But most of Young Lawyer Darrow's cases concerned horses.

"Old Skinflint Brown sold me a pony he swore was hale and hearty," Farmer Harris would complain. "Next morning it dropped dead. I want my money back."

Or, more often, there would be a horse trade. Then a few days afterward, one party or another would claim he had been cheated and demand that the trade be called off. There was nothing like a horse trade to make tempers boil—and in trying to convince the town justice of the peace to decide all sorts of horse cases in favor of his own clients, Lawyer Darrow had fun. However, he did not make much money. Nor, as the months went by, did he feel satisfied.

Then he took a step that improved matters for him greatly. After two years in Andover, he went for a short trip into Pennsylvania, where an old friend had moved. At the home of Jessie Ohl's brother, he and Jessie were married.

Jessie did her best to brighten up the tiny apartment above the shoe shop. But frilly curtains were no real help. The rooms were too small—and Andover itself was too small—for a lawyer to live with his family in comfort. When a year later Jessie presented her husband with a son, Paul, the Darrows were already looking for a new place where they could settle down, for good.

They chose the small city of Ashtabula in the same general area of Ohio. With a population of about five thousand, Ashtabula seemed big enough to offer more of a challenging variety of law cases for Clarence—without overwhelming him.

"I think Clarence feels he has to make a big splash," his sister Jenny explained to their father after visiting in Ashtabula. "That's why he won't take Everett's advice and move to Chicago. I'm sure Clarence is afraid that in Chicago he'd be just a little frog in a big pond."

Jenny was right—for four years. During those four years in Ashtabula, Clarence Darrow gave every sign of being contented with his life as a small-city lawyer. He represented local storekeepers in routine court cases involving small amounts of money. If a housewife ordered a new table from a carpenter, and then refused to pay for it because it did not suit her after all, Darrow might be called on by the carpenter—or by the woman's husband—to appear in court on this weighty matter. He worked on cases involving the selling of farms and the settling of inheritances. There were countless horse-trade cases, too. By this time he was becoming known as a smart young fellow all over Ashtabula.

And he seemed perfectly happy. But discontent was slowly rising within him. His wife sensed it before he did himself.

It began to worry her that he would sit up until all hours reading thick books he kept ordering by mail from Chicago. She could hardly even pronounce the foreign-sounding names of the writers.

"What makes you want to strain your eyes over books by French and Russian people?" she asked impatiently one evening. "They can't tell you anything about Ashtabula."

At that, Darrow smiled a sad little smile. "There is a whole lot more to the world than Ashtabula," he said. "There is a great world where other problems and other ideas . . ." He stopped himself. "I *am* sleepy," he said. "Guess it's time to call it a day."

But his discontent grew steadily, especially after Everett came from Chicago on a visit.

"Clarence, you have too big a brain for a small town," Everett told him as they sat up late together one night. "Come back with me. Move to Chicago."

"But it's an awfully big jump, Ev," Clarence said slowly. "I have only five hundred dollars in the bank. I

don't know a soul but you in Chicago. I'd have to start from scratch again."

"It won't take long to catch on," Everett insisted. "Besides, I have a steady job and I can lend you whatever you need until you get established. You owe it to yourself, Clarence."

Still Clarence refused to move. Indeed, as if fearful that he might be persuaded against his wishes, he began looking for a house to buy in Ashtabula. Up until now, he and his wife and son had been living in a rented house.

Without too much difficulty, they found one they liked that could be bought for $3,500. The owner was a woman. While she was visiting out of town, her husband made an agreement with the Darrows calling for them to pay the five hundred dollars they had in the bank, and the rest of the price in regular monthly payments. When this arrangement was described to the owner, she shook her head.

"I don't think Darrow will be able to keep up the payments," she said.

On being told this, Darrow exploded.

"I don't want your house after all," he told the woman, "because—because I'm going to move away from here."

"Is that so?"

"Yes, I just got a big case. In Chicago!"

Then he had to back up this fib—on the spur of the moment. And so, in 1887, at the age of thirty, Clarence Darrow moved with his family to the great city of Chicago.

4.
N. S. N. F.

Every hour of the day, locomotives clanged into Chicago. From every direction, grain and meat and other farm products came rolling toward this booming center of trade and manufacturing. Every week, new settlers by the hundreds came, too, swelling the population of the exciting city on Lake Michigan up past the one million mark.

On the corner of Madison and State Streets, Chicago's busiest crossroads, a new arrival stood watching the hustle and bustle one morning. He was a big man, a six-footer, but there was nothing stiff about his bearing. In fact, his hands were planted deep in his pockets, and he had the air of a country lawyer about to discuss the case of a stolen milk cow before a local justice of the peace.

His old-fashioned high collar and black bow tie, and his rumpled gray suit, all but proved him a small-towner. Even his broad, friendly face with its open look of trusting everybody suggested that this man was no city dweller at heart.

"Don't know if I'll ever get used to the place," Clarence Darrow muttered to himself. He stared at the people surging by him in every direction, intent on some business of their own, and he shrugged his shoulders. "Who wants a hayseed lawyer like me? I might just as well go off to Brazil, for all they care."

But Darrow did not leave Chicago.

While one part of him fought loneliness and discouragement in the great city, another part began to come alive for the first time. Chicago was filled with people who loved books. Every night of the week, there were meetings and debates on dozens of subjects. The keen minds he discovered thrilled Darrow. Soon he was spending four or five nights a week at some sort of a meeting, listening—and speaking up himself!

"Won't you come along?" he urged his wife. "I'm going to talk at the Single Tax Club tonight."

"You know I'm not interested in taxes," Mrs. Darrow said a little wearily. It had been hard on her, moving away from the calm country life she had always known,

27

into the noise and dirt of Chicago. "I don't see why you can't stay home at night the way you did before," she added.

Darrow's eyebrows lifted, and then he smiled. "If clients won't come to look for me," he said, "I just have to go look for them. One of these days when I make a speech, reporters from the newspapers will take down what I say. Once I get my name in the papers, I won't be just another hayseed lawyer."

Just as Darrow predicted, he *did* get his name into the papers. Among the problems caused by Chicago's rapid growth was one that annoyed him a lot. It was nearly impossible to find a seat on a street car at busy hours because the company had not thought it necessary to increase the number of horse cars in service.

"If they don't give us seats, we shouldn't pay our fares," he fumed to his wife. But Darrow realized that one person alone could not convince the company to change its policy. So he helped to organize a big campaign on the issue—the "N.S.N.F." campaign.

"What is *that?*" Mrs. Darrow asked.

"Very simple," Darrow said. "N.S.N.F. means 'No Seat, No Fare.' We're making thousands of blue ribbon badges with these letters on them in gold. People all over the city will be wearing them. Next month, everybody who gets on a streetcar will refuse to pay the conductor the five-cent fare—unless there are enough vacant seats. I'm speaking at a meeting about this at the Central Music Hall tonight."

Stories about the N.S.N.F. meeting got into the newspaper. Then Darrow was asked to speak at other meetings. He played an important part in making the campaign a success. When the day for refusing to pay arrived, riders by the hundreds refused to give up a nickel unless they got a seat.

"There was quite a fuss," Darrow told his wife. "The police had to be called every few blocks. But the company has come around. They have promised to add more cars during the rush hours."

But despite getting his name into the newspapers, Darrow still had little legal work to do—at first. "People keep coming into my office," he told his wife. "But they don't bring me any law business. They just want to use my telephone—and tell me how the world should be organized so that everybody can have his own telephone." During his whole first year in Chicago, Darrow earned only three hundred dollars. At this rate, he could scarcely pay his own telephone bill. Without Everett's bank account to draw on, he would have had to give up.

But Darrow went right ahead with his debating—and,

finally, his luck changed. One morning a messenger came to his tiny office with a note. The Mayor of Chicago wanted to see Clarence Darrow at City Hall as soon as possible!

"You're sure this isn't a joke?" Darrow asked the messenger.

Having no other business at all on hand, Darrow walked over to the City Hall where, sure enough, Mayor DeWitt Cregier was expecting him. "I want to give you a job on the city's legal staff," Mayor Cregier said. "Ever since I heard you speak on taxes one evening last year, I've been wanting to have you with me. Now there is a job open."

Nor was that the full extent of Darrow's new turn of luck. Within three months after he went to work at City Hall, the assistant head of the city of Chicago's law department resigned—and Darrow got his job. Ten months later, the head of the legal department became so ill that he, too, had to resign. At the age of thirty-three, Clarence Darrow found himself in charge of all the law business of the city of Chicago!

5.

The Turning Point

"All day long people come to me with problems," Darrow told his wife.

Mrs. Darrow was sitting with a basket of mending on her lap. This was one of the few evenings in several weeks that her husband had stayed home after dinner. Seven-year-old Paul had just said good night.

"It's up to me to make decisions on some very complicated matters," Darrow went on. "But I can't take time to look up in the law books to find out how a similar matter was decided somewhere else. So how do you think I manage?"

When his voice paused, Mrs. Darrow was startled. She had not been listening to him talk on and on about his work, and instead was planning what to buy for dinner tomorrow. Fortunately, he did not seem to expect an answer from her.

"I say to myself, 'What is the sensible and honest way for such a matter to be decided?' " he answered himself. "In nine times out of ten, a knotty question can be disposed of without too much difficulty that way." Then Darrow smiled. He was quite aware that his wife had little interest in his work, but still he enjoyed teasing her.

"How would you like it if your husband got rich and famous?" he suddenly asked her.

Mrs. Darrow heard that question. "Clarence, you know I would like to buy a nice house near the lake," she said. "It would be so good for Paul. Now that we've finished paying your brother back, could I start to look for a house?"

Again Darrow smiled a little sadly. If only she would put her mind to something besides houses, he had a serious question he might talk over with her. After two years of working for the city, he was beginning to feel that he could not stay much longer. Politics! He shook his head almost angrily.

"I can't stand the scheming and dickering at City Hall much longer," he told himself. "A political career is not for me. I have to go my own way, on my own." But what way should he take? Maybe he did owe it to Jessie and

Paul to make a lot of money for them. As his wife stitched away, he sat wrapped in thought. The decision he came to astonished his friends.

A few months later, Darrow went to work as a lawyer for the Chicago and North Western Railway. His brother Everett spoke for almost everybody who knew Clarence when he said:

"Clarence, I don't understand it! All your life, you've been jumping to your feet to defend the underdog. You're in favor of anything that will help the poor man get a square deal. Now I'm not saying that there's anything evil about the railroad, but won't it be your job to fight against paying money to railroad workers or passengers who are injured? Won't you have to take the side of the powerful railroad when a poor man claims he got hurt on a train?"

Clarence brushed back the lock of shaggy brown hair that had fallen over his forehead. "I know what you mean, Ev," he said. "But the president of the railroad knows about my feelings. I think it ought to be possible for me to do some good, by helping to smooth the way for a fair settlement when people have some grievance against the railroad."

Everett believed Clarence and no longer feared that his younger brother had changed his sympathies. Other people wondered, though. Had Clarence Darrow decided that making money was more important than defending underdogs? "You can't really blame him," some people said. "After all, by working for the railroad, he can be a rich man in not too long. He'll have a big house by the lake. That's what most people would choose."

It did, indeed, seem to be what Darrow had chosen. Within two years after he went to work for the railroad, he had bought a comfortable house. Mrs. Darrow contentedly hired servants. She even made sure her husband got some new suits, and she had them pressed carefully so that he would no longer look as if he slept in his clothes.

"Darrow is on his way to becoming one of the fat cats of Chicago," his old friends told each other.

Then in the spring of 1894, there came the great turning point of Clarence Darrow's life. The men who built the Pullman sleeping cars that had done so much to increase the comfort of railroad travel decided to stop working. They went out on strike to try to win improved working conditions. And the walkout spread. Other railroad workers supported the strikers. As a lawyer on the payroll of a major railroad, Darrow was expected to help fight the strikers. But he could not do this!

One sultry morning, he marched into the office of his boss—and quit his job.

"You're throwing away a great future," the president of the railroad warned him.

But Darrow's mind was made up. Eugene V. Debs was the leader of the railway workers' union—and Debs was facing jail. Darrow felt deep within his bones that he had to defend Debs.

"These unions can't pay you anything," the president of the Chicago and North Western told Darrow. "When this is over, you'll be stranded, without clients or a future. Stay with us—there's fame and fortune for the asking if you do."

Darrow shook his head. "Then I guess that's not what I want," he said. "*I believe in the right of people to better themselves, and I'm going to throw in my ten cents' worth to help Debs and his union!*"

6.

Conspiracy!

The whole nation was aroused over the railroad strike. Black headlines screamed that the strikers were defying all law and order. President Grover Cleveland sent troops to patrol Chicago's railroad yards. But still freight cars were overturned and burned; three strikers were killed by soldiers' bullets. Eugene V. Debs, the leader of the striking workers, was clapped into jail.

Before visiting Debs in his cell, Darrow went to see the Governor of Illinois. Governor John P. Altgeld was an unusual man. Like Darrow himself, Altgeld believed in fighting for the rights of the poor and oppressed—even when doing so meant standing almost alone. The two had met at an evening debate soon after Darrow's arrival in Chicago, and quickly became close friends. Altgeld still took a fatherly interest in Darrow's career.

"Well, Clarence," Altgeld said, "I hear you resigned from your job to defend Debs. Son, there's little but grief in this martyr business."

Darrow looked quizzically at Altgeld, who had just risked his own reputation by protesting to President Cleveland about the sending of Federal soldiers to Chicago—on the grounds that they were causing, rather than preventing, violence.

"You know, Governor," Darrow said, "most men do things through a desire to escape pain. Did you ever stop and watch a blind man begging on a street corner? A man passes by hurriedly and suddenly stops still. He goes back and drops a coin in the blind man's cup. The sight of the helpless man standing forlornly at a corner hurts him, makes him feel a sense of social responsibility, and so he buys ten cents' worth of relief from social pain. It hurts me too much to see Debs and men like him faced with the possibility of spending years in prison, so I am buying relief, too."

For Darrow refused to accept the widely-held opinion that Debs was a "dangerous monster." In newspapers and even from the pulpits of some churches, that is how the strike leader was being described. But to Darrow, Debs was—a hero!

In Darrow's eyes, the strike by the railroad workers

was completely justified. He believed that the workmen on the payroll of the Pullman Company had had every right to quit work in protest, after their pay had been cut four times within a year.

"There are skilled men who had been making $3.20 a day last year—and, at that, they barely made ends meet," Darrow told Altgeld. "Now the same men are supposed to feed their families *on only $1.20 a day!*"

Darrow not only believed that the workmen had a just grievance against their bosses, but he also believed that they had chosen a sensible way to press for better treatment. *"The men have every right to join together in a union,"* he declared.

However, to many other people in 1894, there was something suspicious about labor unions—and when a union took any forceful step to try to win higher wages or shorter hours, the situation seemed outright alarming.

In the case of this railroad strike, the alarm had mounted higher and higher—because the workers for a whole industry had joined together. Eugene V. Debs had formed a big union composed of engineers and clerks, firemen and conductors, working for railroads all over the country. And this union was supporting the Pullman workers.

Thus, pickets were preventing trains that carried Pullman cars from entering or leaving Chicago. They were doing so peacefully, union men and their sympathizers insisted. "Whatever violence there has been comes from hoodlums hired by the railroads to break the strike," Darrow told Altgeld.

But in the hot-tempered atmosphere brought on by the strike, the lawyer stood little chance of freeing Debs —and he knew it.

"They have the cards stacked against us, Gene," Darrow told Debs when he visited the union leader in his cell.

Debs, a mild, bald man, who had started life in a small Indiana city where his parents kept a grocery store, did not look the part of a "dangerous monster." He nodded quietly.

"It's that blamed conspiracy thing!" Darrow said, getting up to pace back and forth a few steps. "The way the law now stands in the United States of America, if a boy steals a dime, a small fine covers the offense; he can't be sent to the penitentiary. But if two boys *agree* to steal a dime, they are guilty of conspiracy. Both of them can be sent to the penitentiary as conspirators. And you're a 'conspirator,' Gene."

Darrow lounged back against the wall and stuck his thumbs into his suspenders.

"The law says it's all right to join a union," he went on,

as if thinking aloud. "Fine! But now take the case of a workman who doesn't like the idea of working twelve hours a day for less than a dollar and a half. He goes to his boss and demands a raise. That's legal, although it probably won't do him a bit of good. The boss can fire him and that's that.

"Then let a whole group of workmen, a union, go to a boss and demand shorter hours. Ah! Now we have a conspiracy afoot. Furthermore, suppose that someone swears he saw a striker throw a torch on a railroad car. What difference if the witness is a low character hired as a spy by the railroad managers' association? Now we have a conspiracy to destroy railroad property. That's a prison offense—and that's what they're out to get you for. But I'll do the best I can, Gene."

What Darrow did was to try a bold maneuver. He tried to use the conspiracy law for his own ends—claiming it was the railroad managers who had been guilty of conspiracy.

"They have conspired to deprive honest workmen of fair wages," he insisted. "They have conspired to force down wages until skilled workers face starvation."

Darrow took the Debs case all the way to the United States Supreme Court—and lost. But although he lost, in a larger sense he won. Before many more decades had passed, the rights of American workmen that Darrow had defended in this case would be guaranteed by law. Darrow's leadership in a peaceful revolution would bring him honor. But for the time being, he was a man without a job.

7.

Widows and Orphans

Again Darrow put his name on the door of a law office in Chicago. But unlike the dreary time right after he had arrived in the city, almost immediately he had more business than he could handle. For the word had spread.

"There's a lawyer fellow who threw up a good job with the railroad to try to help Debs," a poor, Polish-born steel worker told his brother, who had just been gypped of his life's savings by a scheming storekeeper. "Go see Darrow."

"If you need help in getting the pension you're entitled to," a woman whose husband had just died was advised by her parish priest, "go see a lawyer named Darrow."

And soon the hall outside of Darrow's office was clogged with people waiting to see him. Some of them had so little money that they could not pay him a fee;

even so, he helped as many as he could. In the city courthouse, one judge told another: "Clarence Darrow has more widows and orphans for clients than all of the other lawyers in Chicago put together!"

Before half-past eight every morning, Darrow came ambling into his office with the most relaxed and easy-going air. Despite Mrs. Darrow's best efforts, his clothes still looked as if he slept in them. And stuffed into a pocket of his jacket was the apple or bunch of grapes that would be his lunch. From breakfast onward, he was usually too busy to stop and eat more than this—sometimes until late in the evening.

Listening to a client talk about his troubles, Darrow would sink down so low in his desk chair that it seemed almost as if he was sitting on his neck. But this was no sign of his not being interested. On the contrary! Clarence Darrow's keen mind somehow worked best when he looked laziest.

Occasionally, he would astonish even other lawyers who knew how good his memory was, by telling a courtroom a whole long and complicated story about an insurance policy word for word as he had heard it in his office when he had looked practically asleep. And he was able to pick out the important details in a poor widow's long tale of woe.

But not all of his business dealt with the hardships of the poor. He also began to defend people accused of crimes—he felt that anybody but a hardened criminal deserved his best efforts. In addition, he was sought after more and more by labor unions.

"I know you will be told that I am a labor agitator or a Socialist," Darrow told a jury in Oshkosh, Wisconsin. He was there to defend the officers of a woodworkers' union against a conspiracy charge. They were accused of conspiring to reduce the profits of a window frame factory —by going out on strike for shorter hours.

"But I appeal to you," said Darrow, "on behalf of those men who rise in the morning before daylight comes and who go home at night when the light has faded from the sky . . . on behalf of those who give their life, their strength, their toil to make others rich and great."

The jury was touched by his appeal. Their verdict was —"Not guilty!" This decision was Darrow's first major victory in a labor union case.

But besides all of his legal business, Darrow still found time to keep on with his debating in the evenings. He spent so little time at home that, in 1897, he and his wife decided it no longer made sense for them to live together. They were divorced, but although fourteen-year-old Paul went to live with his mother, Darrow spent many a weekend with his son. They often went for walks in the country, or on fishing trips.

Darrow himself took an apartment with a fellow lawyer, and for several years their bachelor quarters was a magnet for writers, artists and scientists. The most interesting people in Chicago came there to talk over the news of the day, or to discuss a new Russian novel. Then Darrow met a red-headed newspaperwoman named Ruby Hamerstrom, who was engaged to another man.

"You can't really mean to marry someone else," Darrow told her firmly. "You ought to marry me." In July of 1903, when Darrow was forty-six and Ruby thirty, they were married. Despite the difference in their ages, this was a very happy marriage. The second Mrs. Darrow had a lively mind and she enjoyed meetings and debates just as much as her husband did—although she let him do the talking for the family. Indeed, she stopped working after their marriage so that she could devote all of her time to her husband and his career.

She was a wonderful hostess. Soon she found a handsome apartment on the street called the Midway, near the University of Chicago—a large and airy apartment with enormous windows giving a wide view of the city. Here she entertained at dinner parties where the conversation was fascinating and the food delicious—even if a large number of common dishes could never be served. For Darrow himself was a finicky eater, who even objected to watching other people eat what he disliked.

"He won't touch any chicken, turkey, lamb or veal," Mrs. Darrow told the maid who helped her. "We can't have any onions, cabbage, celery, spinach, tomatoes or green beans, either. But he does like pies and cake."

As much as the new Mrs. Darrow loved their comfortable apartment on the Midway, she was still willing to pack up at a moment's notice and leave town with her husband. This was fortunate, because Darrow was now being invited to give lectures in many cities. What is more, he was becoming famous as a lawyer. By winning several important labor union cases, he was gaining a reputation as the nation's leading labor lawyer. When an important union case came up anywhere in the country, he was bound to be called on. Late in 1905, a very important case came up in Idaho!

8.

Miners and Murderers

It was the afternoon of December 30, 1905, in Caldwell, Idaho. Former Governor Frank Steunenberg started home from his office at the usual time. Then, as usual, he stopped off in the local hotel, to buy a newspaper and chat a while with friends. As he sat in the lobby reading and chatting, a stranger watched him.

When Steunenberg stood up, the stranger casually rose, too. Steunenberg walked out of the front door of the hotel and strolled down the block toward his own home. Meanwhile, the plump, red-faced stranger hurried upstairs to his hotel room, then out the back way and across the snow-covered fields.

As former Governor Steunenberg walked in at his own front gate, he kicked a piece of string that was in his way.

A stick of dynamite had been attached to this. An explosion came a second later—and it killed him. By this time, the plump, red-faced stranger was back at the hotel, sipping a glass of beer at the bar.

"Whatever can that noise be?" the stranger named Harry Orchard innocently asked the bartender.

Thus started a wild two years for Clarence Darrow.

He was called in to defend a group of union leaders accused of engineering the murder. For the killing of the former governor was immediately linked to the vicious war that had been going on in the Rocky Mountain states between miners and mine owners. This had started when the miners demanded better working conditions. Not only did the owners refuse, but they also fired union leaders for being troublemakers.

Both the miners and the owners were rough, tough men. Dynamite was in common use in the area. Soon a silver mine here, and a copper mine there was being blasted into rubble—and miners, whether innocent or guilty of the dynamitings, were herded into barbed-wire camps. During his term as governor, Frank Steunenberg had made himself a prime target of the miners' hate—and so it seemed logical to many people that miners must have murdered him. But what about the plump, red-faced stranger?

In short order, he was arrested. He had not even left town. He had not even thrown away the string and dynamite in a box under the bed in his hotel room. And no sooner did police question him than he confessed *that three mine union leaders had hired him to do the killing.*

"Is that so?" Darrow said sarcastically when he arrived in Idaho. "Whose word do we have about this? A convicted criminal who admits that he murdered for hire. He's the scum of the earth, this Harry Orchard is."

Then through a series of trials that lasted two years, Darrow drummed away at one idea. The mine owners had wanted to discredit the union once and for all, he claimed. *So the owners and not the miners had hired Orchard.*

And part of the bargain, he said, was that Orchard had to be arrested—in order to "confess." Then, although he would have to be kept in jail for many years, he would be given a private apartment and many other special privileges.

Defending the miners in an impassioned speech, Darrow spoke in court for eleven hours—without once referring to any written notes. He gave the whole history of the war in the mining industry. Even people who thought he was a dangerous radical were held spellbound. He spoke as if effortlessly, but only a master speaker could

have moved the hearts of his hearers as he did when he
said to the jury:

"I speak for the poor, for the weak, for the weary, for
that long line of men who, in darkness and despair, have
borne the labors of the human race. Their eyes are upon
you twelve men of Idaho tonight . . ."

The jury's verdict was—that the miners were "not
guilty!"

But then other related cases against the union officials
were pressed, and Darrow's health broke under the
strain. He had such severe pains in one ear that he had
to go into a hospital, and yet doctors could not find the
cause of the trouble. For many weeks, he lay close to
death.

He recovered—to face a fantastic series of new ups and
downs.

Returning to Chicago, Darrow was treated like a king
by the plain people of the city. He could no longer sit
munching peanuts in the bleachers and watching the
Chicago Cubs play ball on a Saturday afternoon. Too
many people crowded close to watch him instead of the
ball game. He could scarcely walk down a street without
being mobbed by people who wanted to shake his hand.

Then from the heights of fame, Darrow plunged down
to disgrace.

The swift descent came as the result of a spectacular case in Los Angeles. Here two brothers who were union officers had been accused of dynamiting the plant of the Los Angeles *Times*, causing a fire that killed twenty printers. Since Darrow was the nation's foremost labor lawyer, the McNamara brothers sought him to defend them. Not only their own lives, but also the reputation of the whole union movement was at stake. Union men in every part of the country believed the McNamaras had been "framed" in an effort to discredit unionism. It was up to Darrow to prove this.

But as he investigated, he became more and more convinced that *the McNamaras were guilty as charged.* He was sure they would be convicted. Coming to the hardest decision he had ever made, he told them:

"You are going to hang. I cannot save you. But if you will tell the truth, you will get a prison term. I advise you to change your plea from 'not guilty' to 'guilty'—not only to save your lives, but to play fair with the union movement. The truth is bound to come out in the course of the trial. And when it does, the fact that you lied will give all union men a worse black eye than if you tell the truth now."

The McNamaras agreed to take their lawyer's advice. When court convened the next morning, Darrow rose and said quietly: "Your Honor, my clients wish to change their plea from 'not guilty' to 'guilty.'" Some people were not listening carefully. But as Darrow sat down, reporters raced for telephones. The judge rapped in vain for order.

And within a few hours, people all over America who had loved Clarence Darrow were speaking his name with scorn.

"Traitor!" they called him.

For they could not believe that the McNamaras really had been guilty as charged. They could not help believing that Darrow had "sold out" to interests that wanted to discredit unionism. Nor was this scorn all that Darrow had to bear.

Within a few days, he himself was charged with committing a crime. *The eminent Clarence Darrow was accused of bribing jurors.* He was charged with arranging, through an intermediary, to pay thousands of dollars to men on the jury in the McNamara case—if they would vote to acquit his clients. Despite Darrow's insistence that his whole career proved he would never even think of such a thing, he was tried, twice. On one set of charges he was judged not guilty; on a second set, a jury could not agree. Finally, all of the charges against Darrow were dismissed—but he was a broken man.

"Rube," he told his wife, "it kinda looks like our lawyering days are over."

Many of his former friends seemed to have deserted him. Even the plain people he had helped so much no longer wanted him to defend them in court. No matter if he had or had not bribed jurors, they thought he probably had been guilty of some shady practices. "Where there's so much smoke, there must have been fire," they said. And so Darrow, at fifty-six, found himself penniless —with no work to do.

He took to lecturing for money, and people paid to hear him speak. Then gradually, the old magic began to come back. Some had never stopped believing in Darrow's honesty; slowly others changed their minds about him, and within a few years he was again practicing law. Now most of his cases were defending people accused of crimes from forgery to murder. During the First World War, he defended many men jailed for refusing to fight because their consciences forbade killing. Darrow built up an amazing record of convincing juries of the innocence of his clients. But the most amazing case of his whole career was still to come.

9.

The Monkey Trial

Sixty-eight-year-old Clarence Darrow was lecturing about the causes of crime in Richmond, Virginia. Although his shaggy hair was gray now, a lock of it still kept falling over his forehead when he leaned over the speaker's stand—just as in his youth. But now he tired more easily.

"Well, Rube," he said to his wife as they were leaving the meeting, "I won't mind a bit going home." They had been on a lecture trip for several weeks; now, in 1925, Darrow spent much of his time speaking and writing.

But the Darrows did not go right back to Chicago. A story on the front page of the afternoon newspapers changed his mind. The papers reported that in the small town of Dayton, Tennessee, a high school science teacher named John Scopes had been arrested—and charged with a surprising crime.

He was accused of teaching his students that not every word in the Bible was absolutely true.

"It's turning back the clock to the Dark Ages," Darrow grunted as he read the paper. "I'd like to take some part in that trial." And so, instead of going back to Chicago, Darrow and his wife went to Tennessee.

John Scopes welcomed them eagerly. And many thoughtful people everywhere took heart when the famous lawyer ambled off a train in Dayton on a hot, sticky July afternoon. For even before the Scopes trial started, it was a world sensation.

The very thought that in the twentieth century, in the enlightened United States, it could be considered a crime to teach children a widely-accepted scientific theory— had shocked people everywhere. But signs of trouble had been appearing for some time.

In several states, Fundamentalists objected strongly to science books that taught children the ideas of the great English scientist, Charles Darwin. Back in the middle years of the nineteenth century, Darwin had worked out his *theory of evolution.* It stated that life on earth had started millions of years ago with tiny, one-celled creatures, and that, gradually, more complicated animals developed. Then slowly, from the same far-distant ancestor, there had developed the various families of monkeys— and man.

Many religious people had come to accept Darwin's theory of evolution without being disturbed by the differences between his theory and the story of man's creation as told in the Bible.

But the Fundamentalists believed that the Bible must be accepted *word for word*. Therefore, they felt that Darwin was in grave error. In Tennessee, the Fundamentalists had recently succeeded in having a law passed that made it a crime to talk about the Theory of Evolution in any classroom in the state!

Now John Scopes had been arrested and the new law would have its first test.

Moreover, one of the most famous of living Americans had volunteered his services to put the case *against* Scopes. This made it doubly urgent to Clarence Darrow that Scopes be well defended.

The prosecutor in the case was William Jennings Bryan. Three times Bryan had run for President on the Democratic ticket, and three times he had been defeated. But even those who had never voted for him admitted he was a spellbinding speaker. An old man now, in recent years he had been devoting his strength to ridiculing Darwin.

"I will pay one hundred dollars in cash to anybody who will sign a paper saying that he personally is descended from an ape," Bryan had shouted at meeting after meeting.

Meanwhile, Darrow had never ceased speaking out in favor of free speech and free thought. And so the stage in Dayton was set for a battle of giants—in a circus atmosphere.

Thousands of people milled around the courthouse when the trial started. Hot dog stands were everywhere, doing a rush business. So were peddlers selling banners and buttons that said: "Your Old Man's a Monkey!" Or, more politely, "READ YOUR BIBLE."

Popular opinion in Dayton was strongly for Bryan and the anti-evolutionists. Even the judge made no secret of how much he disapproved of young Mr. Scopes and his lawyers. Darrow himself was in despair as time after time his efforts to get the testimony of respected scientists onto the record was turned down. Then he had an inspiration.

"If I can't get my scientists on the stand to give expert evidence about evolution," he told his wife, "then maybe

I can get an 'expert' on the Bible to blow up his own case."

And that is exactly what Darrow did—in a courtroom scene that has gone down in history.

Darrow requested William Jennings Bryan himself to take the witness stand. Bryan was vain enough to enjoy being described as an expert on the Bible—even by his opponent. So he willingly agreed. Then Darrow casually leaned an elbow on the railing around the witness stand. Some of the jurors grinned, noticing that his elbow had poked through a hole in his shirt sleeve. (It was so hot that all of the men had shed their jackets.) Then, with a careless, folksy kind of drawl, Darrow proceeded to demolish William Jennings Bryan—and his whole argument.

"I know there are millions of people in the world who derive consolation from the Bible," Darrow said in a statement of his own. "If anybody finds anything in this life that brings them consolation and health and happiness I think they ought to have it. But the Bible is not one book. It is made up of sixty-six books written over a period of about a thousand years, some of them very early and some of them comparatively late. It is a book primarily of religion and morals. It is not a book of science. Never was and never was meant to be."

Then he turned to Bryan.

"You have given considerable study to the Bible, haven't you, Mr. Bryan?" he asked.

"Yes, I have. I have studied the Bible for about fifty years."

"Do you claim that everything in the Bible should be literally interpreted?"

"I believe that everything in the Bible should be accepted as it is given there."

Darrow hitched his thumbs into his purple suspenders. "When you read that the whale swallowed Jonah," he said, "how do you literally interpret that?" A murmur of surprise arose.

"When I read that a big fish swallowed Jonah, I believe it," Bryan said, "and I believe in a God who can make a big fish and make a man and make them both do what He pleases. One miracle is just as easy to believe as another."

"You mean just as hard."

"It is hard to believe for you, but easy for me."

Darrow raised an eyebrow, then went on: "Do you believe Joshua made the sun stand still?"

"I believe what the Bible says."

"If you believe that the sun stood still then you must agree that the earth also stood still?"

"I don't know . . ."

"Now, Mr. Bryan, have you ever pondered what would have happened to the earth if it stood still suddenly?"

"No."

"Don't you know it would have been converted into a molten mass of matter?"

"I don't think about things I don't think about." As even the friendly audience in the court began to laugh at him, Bryan glared. But now the damage was done. Hammering away with one scientific question after another, Darrow proved that Bryan had no knowledge at all about the dates when various early civilizations thrived, or about any scientific discoveries. And so his contention that the Bible was absolutely true could not be taken seriously.

When Bryan stepped down, his case was lost—even though the Dayton jury decided that Scopes was guilty. Within a few months, this verdict was reversed by a higher court—as many had expected after Darrow's masterful performance. By winning this important case, Clarence Darrow greatly advanced the cause of freedom of thought.

10.

The Old Lion

Darrow tried to retire after the Scopes trial. He and his wife had loved traveling, and had fit several trips to Europe into his busy schedule. But now he yearned to take a really long vacation in Switzerland, and there were so many other places he wanted to see.

"Then when we come home, Rube, I want to devote my time to the questions that interest me most," he told his wife. "After nearly fifty years of practicing law, it will be a relief to be able to speak and write, or rest, just as I please."

But things were not to work out quite that way. Every day the mail brought new appeals for help, and there were some cases he could not bring himself to turn down. From Detroit, a group of Negroes appealed to him. They were being held on a murder charge, after firing on a white mob that had been storming the home of a Negro doctor who had just moved into a white neighborhood. "When it comes to people, I am color blind," Darrow often said. He took the case, and was able to get the murder charge dismissed.

Then Darrow and his wife did leave for a long tour of Europe. By then, Darrow had celebrated his fiftieth anniversary as a lawyer—in 1928—and he had enough money to live on comfortably without working anymore. The money was invested in a gas company that his son, Paul, was managing out in Denver, Colorado. Now it really seemed that Darrow had made good on his promise to retire.

From Switzerland, Darrow wrote playful letters to his three granddaughters in Denver. To twelve-year-old Mary, he wrote:

> Eye tak mi penn in hand two let U no that Eye am wel and hop U.R. the sam. Eye kant rite very mutch bekaus it is ten oklok an Eye must do sum worruk.
>
> *Ur Grand Dad*

The "worruk" was dictating the story of his life to his wife. Over the years, Darrow had written many articles and also several books about his ideas on crime and punishment. Now he was putting together his memories—and this book became a best seller. Darrow, with his shaggy hair and lumbering walk, was known affectionately to newspaper readers everywhere as "The Old Lion." Now readers by the thousands bought his book to see what The Old Lion had to say about himself.

But the nickname was not really too apt. For, in his book as in life, Darrow did not roar. He spoke out his thoughts, sometimes teasingly, sometimes very seriously, but he did not roar at people. He believed in trying to convince people by appealing to their reason and to their finer feelings, not by trying to frighten them. But he was not always very complimentary, either.

The chairman of a meeting in Miami introduced him to the audience by saying: "It gives me great pleasure to present Mr. Darrow to such a large and intelligent audience."

Darrow got to his feet and glanced silently out at the six hundred people waiting to hear him speak. He shook his head. "My friend, the chairman, is mistaken," he finally said. "There are not this many intelligent people in the whole world."

But fortunately people in every important city were delighted to pay money to listen to him. For in the Great

Depression of 1929, Darrow lost all of his savings. Paul's gas company failed, and Darrow had to earn his living again. He chose to earn it by debating about religion all over the United States. In every city he visited, he argued the case for being a non-believer—against a local minister, priest and rabbi. More often than not, they all parted excellent friends.

Indeed, one prominent minister, after debating with Darrow, said: "Of all the men I have ever known—men rich or poor, literate or illiterate, conservative, liberal or radical—I would rank Darrow with Gandhi of India as the gentlest. Darrow finds it easy to forgive his enemies, and love them, for he has great mercy on them."

After speaking out in favor of unpopular causes for more than half a century, Darrow had become widely hated, it is true, but even more widely loved. Even people who disagreed with his ideas believed he had done his country a great service—by fighting to protect the rights of the weak and underprivileged.

At the age of seventy-seven, Darrow was called to Washington by President Franklin D. Roosevelt—and, as the nation's outstanding liberal lawyer, was asked to review some New Deal laws designed to help small businessmen. Proving that he had not lost his old fire, Darrow sharply criticized some features of the new laws.

But now he tired too easily for any continued effort. After a last sentimental visit to Kinsman, he took to the big brass bed in his Chicago apartment with its enormous windows. There was a big marble-topped table beside his bed, piled with books. Sometimes he read; sometimes he dictated articles to his wife, about his boyhood, or about subjects of current interest; sometimes he merely gazed out of the windows, watching the sun rise or set. On March 13, 1938, when he was one month short of his eighty-first birthday, he died.

Then all Chicago turned out to do him honor. For forty-eight hours, the people of the city filed past his coffin to bid him farewell. Thousands who could not fit into the University of Chicago chapel where his funeral was held stood outside in a pouring rain, just to pay him their last respects. In keeping with his own wishes, his body was cremated and the ashes scattered to the wind by his son Paul. "But what he did for America," the newspapers said, "will never be forgotten."